This book is dedicated to Mrs. Johnson.

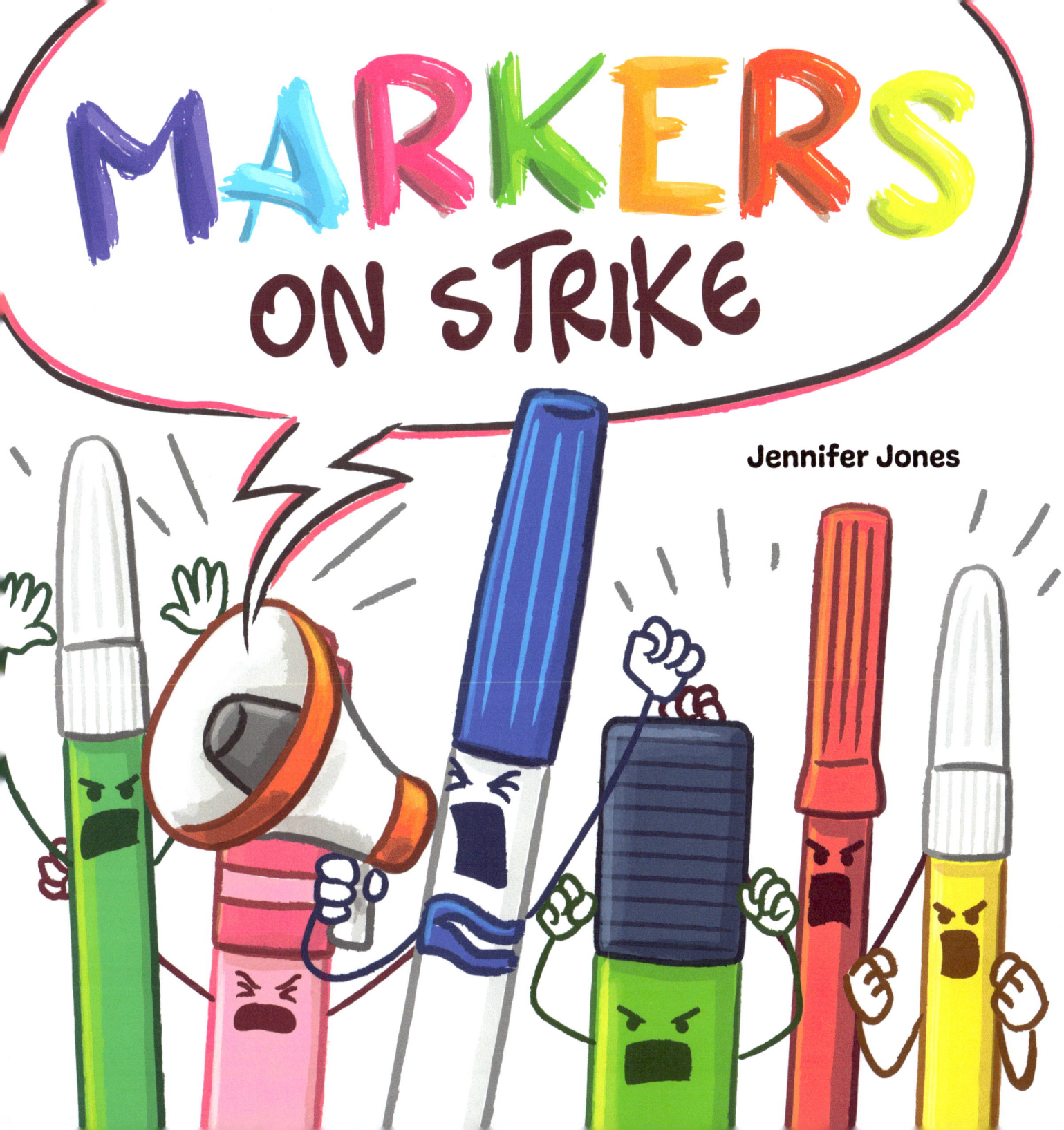

When most people think of markers,
they think of color, brightness, and joy.
We're tools for creativity,
maybe your favorite pastime toy.

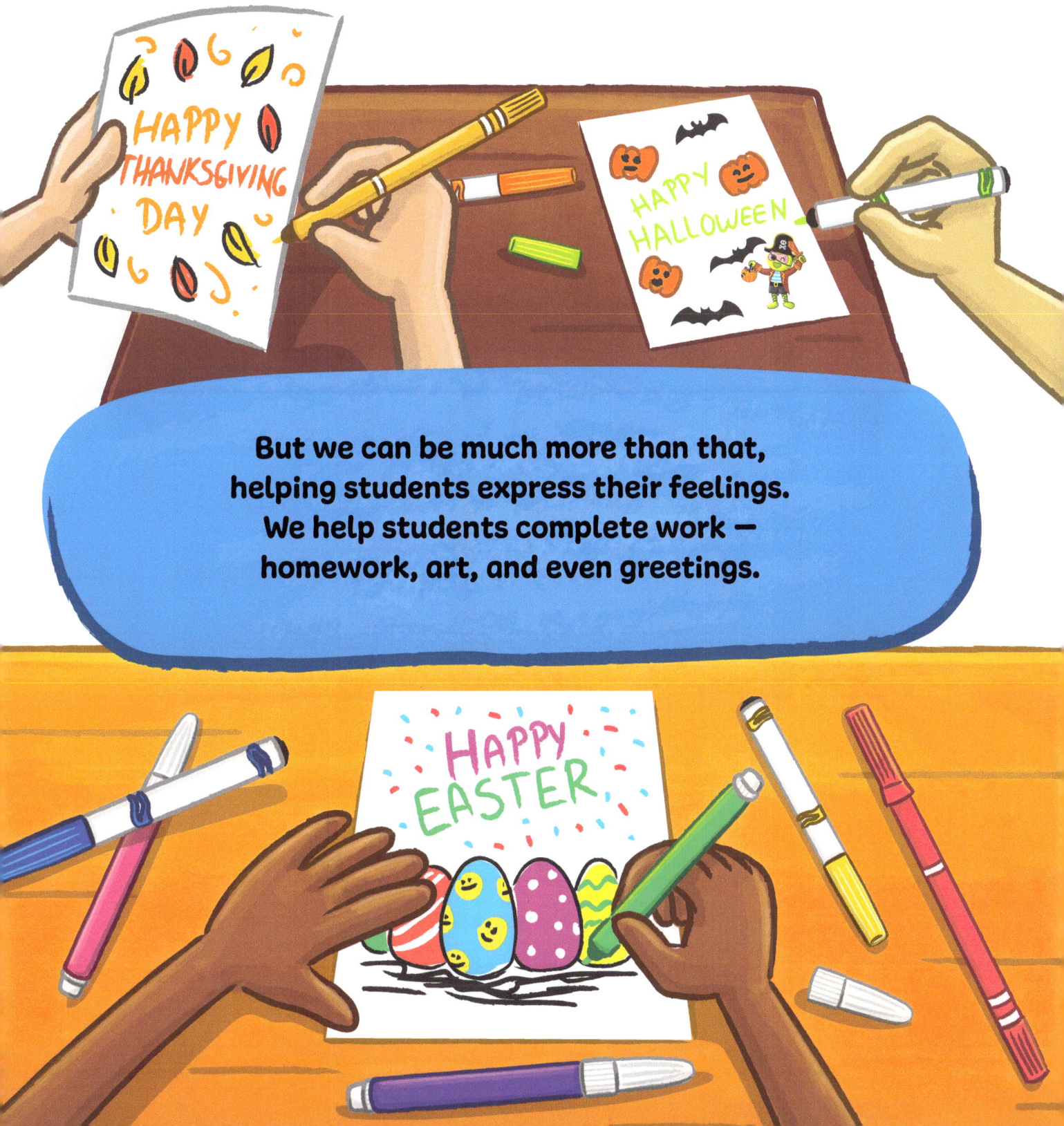

But we can be much more than that, helping students express their feelings. We help students complete work — homework, art, and even greetings.

We color up students' pages
with rainbows big and bright.
Without us, students would stare upon
blank pages filled only with white.

So you'd think the students would treat us right,
with caution and with care.
But they don't! They make us wish
that we weren't even there.

**Well, we were tired of being treated poorly.
We were especially fed up one night,
so we grabbed a piece of paper,
and, we, the markers, began to write...**

Dear students, we're tired of being treated poorly.
It's not something we like.
We've decided we've had enough,
and we are going on strike!

You chisel our tips and grind us down

until our fronts are no more than stumps.

As you smoosh us across the paper,

we're forced to leave behind yucky clumps.

You chew our caps with your mouths, covering us in your drool.

Is this how you treat other supplies you're required to use at school?

You bend us and you snap us,
so we can no longer be used.
Do you have any idea what it feels like
to be so often abused?

You mix us together in bins

instead of putting us back in our box.

You use us on things that aren't paper

like the top of your desks or playground rocks.

The worst is when you leave our tops off,
so that we just dry out and die.
Would you treat others like this?
It makes us want to cry.

We see you laugh and giggle

as you carelessly put on the wrong tops.

It makes us sad and angry.

We probably should call the cops.

So the next time that you need us,

we WON'T be there to assist.

We are going on strike!

We don't even know if we'll be missed..

The students walked into their class the next day.
Something was missing, but what?
One noticed the letter sticking out of the marker box,
stopping it from closing shut.

When they couldn't find us,
they grabbed some paper to write us back
but they couldn't even write in color.
No, they had to use a boring shade of black.

We promise not to chew your ends

or snap you, as you said.

We'll use you for art and schoolwork,

creatively and carefully instead!

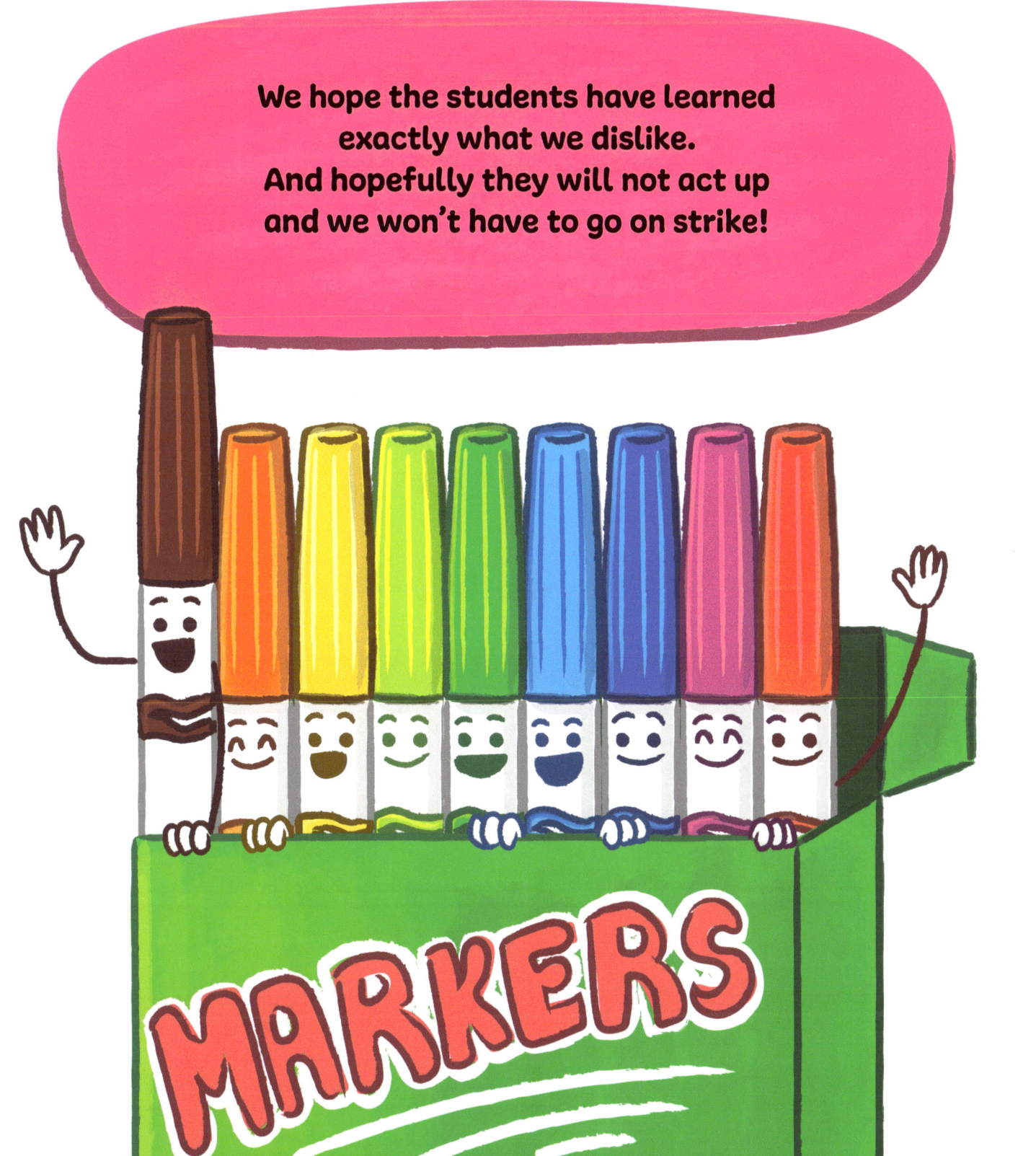

www.ingramcontent.com/pod-product-compliance
Lightning Source LLC
Chambersburg PA
CBHW041523070526
44585CB00002B/57